Dover Publications, Inc.
Garden City, New York

Twelve beautifully rendered dinosaurs are featured in this collection of safe and temporary tattoos. They are also waterproof. Dinosaurs are identified by number (cut away numbers before applying tattoos): (1) Tyrannosaurus Rex; (2) Utahraptor; (3) Gastonia; (4) Stegosaurus; (5) Liliensternus; (6) Argentinosaurus; (7) Albertosaurus; (8) Apatosaurus; (9) Hypsilophodon; (10) Urodromeus; (11) Centrosaurus; (12) Tylocephale.

Copyright

Copyright © 1999 by Dover Publications, Inc.
All rights reserved.

Bibliographical Note

Mini Dinosaurs Tattoos is a new work, first published by Dover Publications, Inc., in 1999.

International Standard Book Number
ISBN-13: 978-0-486-40772-2
ISBN-10: 0-486-40772-1

Manufactured in the United States by TemporaryTattoos.com
40772116   2020
www.doverpublications.com

MiNi DiNOSAURS TaTToos

JaN SOVaK

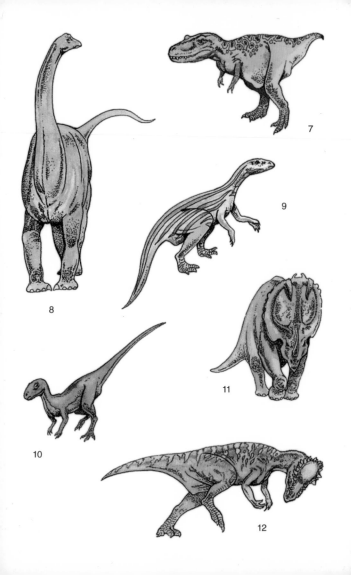

7

9

8

11

10

12

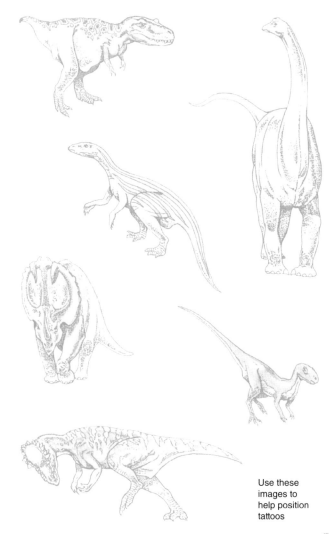

Use these images to help position tattoos

Use these images to help position tattoos

CT986288